HITCHCOCK POSTER ART

FROM THE MARK H. WOLFF COLLECTION
EDITED BY TONY NOURMAND AND MARK H. WOLFF

ART DIRECTION AND DESIGN BY GRAHAM MARSH
TEXT BY MARK H. WOLFF

THE OVERLOOK PRESS
Woodstock • New York

First published in the United States in 1999 by
The Overlook Press, Peter Mayer Publishers, Inc.
Lewis Hollow Road
Woodstock, New York 12498

ISBN: 0-87951-714-X

1 3 5 7 9 8 6 4 2

A CIP catalog record of this book is available from
The Library of Congress

Page make-up by Trevor Gray
Text edited by Roxanna Haijani

Printed in Singapore by C.S. Graphics

ACKNOWLEDGEMENTS

Wayne Beach
Dominque Besson
Lee Brinsmead
Joe Burtis
Glyn Callingham
Jean-Louis Capitaine
Morris Everett, Jr.
Leslie Gardner
Jean-Pierre Giangrande
Mike Hawks
Sam Irvin
Peter Langs
Bruce Merchant
John Myhre
Gabrielle Pantucci
Walter Reuben
Wendy Rubin
Sam Sarowitz
Dan Strebin
Ken Taylor
X-Man

Front Cover:
Psycho (1960)
Paramount
British 30 x 40 in. (76 x 102 cm) (Style B)

Back Cover:
The Birds/Psycho (Ptaci/Psycho) (c.1960s)
Universal
Czech 33 x 23 in. (84 x 58 cm)

The Reel Poster Gallery
72 Westbourne Grove
London W2 5SH
Tel: +44 (0) 171 727 4488
Fax: +44 (0) 171 727 4499

Web Site: www.reelposter.com
Email: info@reelposter.com

Hitchcock had Alma; I had Alison. MARK H. WOLFF

Alfred & Alma Hitchcock working on the screenplay for **Shadow Of A Doubt** (1942).

CONTENTS

INTRODUCTION

This book is my way of paying homage to my favourite cinematic storyteller, a misunderstood genius who was too entertaining during his lifetime to be considered a serious artist. Only now, a generation after his death, has Hitchcock been recognized as a brilliant filmmaker: a bravura technical innovator with a virtuoso visual style.

Suspense, irony and light humour belie the complex moral sense of his films. Moreover, he was uniquely adaptable: no other director has ever made three successive masterpieces as remarkably dissimilar as **Vertigo**, **North By Northwest** and **Psycho**? Pauline Kael dubbed him 'the master entertainer of the movie medium'. The Hitchcock touch is unmistakable. Let's celebrate his centennial by enjoying his legacy: for, as he himself said, 'All that matters, all that exists for the audience, is what is on the screen.'

MARK H. WOLFF

Cahiers Du Cinema (No. 39) (October 1954).
The first issue highlighting Alfred Hitchcock.

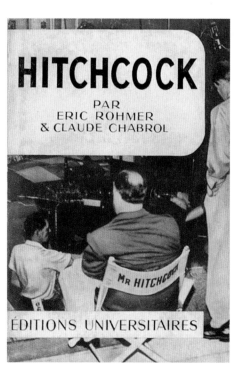

'**Hitchcock**' by Eric Rohmer & Claude Chabrol:
Editions Universitaires, 1957.
The first book written on Alfred Hitchcock.

'**Hitchcock: Truffaut**': **Edition Definitive** –
French Edition, 1983.

'Life' Magazine Cover (1st February 1963)   Photograph by Philippe Halsman.

A HUNDRED YEARS OF HITCHCOCK

Alfred Joseph Hitchcock was born on 13 August 1899, in Leytonstone, an eastern suburb of London, and studied art at the University of London. He began his career in 1919 designing title cards for silent films at Paramount's Famous Players-Lasky studio in London. Over the next few years he acquired various filmmaking skills, such as editing, scripting and art direction and, in 1925, directed his first feature film, **The Pleasure Garden**. This directorial debut was followed by several impressive and important films between 1925 and 1934 including **The Lodger** (1927), and the first British talkie, **Blackmail** (1929). It was, however, **The Man Who Knew Too Much** (1934) which began to earn Hitchcock an international reputation; a reputation which was enhanced in the late 1930s by a number of superb thrillers including **The 39 Steps** (1935), **The Secret Agent** (1936), **Sabotage** (1936) and **The Lady Vanishes** (1938).

In 1940, Hitchcock was invited to America by the renowned Hollywood producer, David O. Selznick, to direct **Rebecca**. Based on Daphne du Maurier's novel, **Rebecca** was the only Hitchcock film to win an Academy Award for Best Picture. During the 1940s, Hitchcock further explored the dynamics of evil and deception in a series of psychological dramas. These included **Suspicion** (1941), **Shadow Of A Doubt** (1943), **Spellbound** (1945) and **Notorious** (1946). He demonstrated his technical wizardry in **Lifeboat** (1944) by restricting the entire action to the confines of a small boat. In **Rope** (1948),

Hitchcock tried to create a film which appeared to have been shot in a single unedited take.

It is the 1950s, however, which are regarded by many as Hitchcock's finest decade; his art reached its full maturity with thrillers such as **Strangers On A Train** (1951), **Dial M For Murder** (1954), **Rear Window** (1954), **Vertigo** (1958), **North By Northwest** (1959) and **Psycho** (1960), which many regard as his last masterpiece.

When I was approached by Mark Wolff in the summer of 1998 to explore the possibility of compiling a homage to Alfred Hitchcock, I was excited at the opportunity to document the imagery that accompanied the films of this master director. With items from various countries, Mark has the most comprehensive collection of Hitchcock memorabilia known to exist. Much of his collection consists of previously unseen, one-of-a-kind items; in this book we have focused on the film posters and lobby cards from Mark's collection. In making our selection, we have tried to include as wide as possible a range of images, juxtaposing the rare and unfamiliar with the better-known.

I hope that this book can be used by students, cinephiles and collectors as an alternative source of reference. I also hope that the posters will continue to serve the purpose for which they were originally designed, and seduce a new generation of movie-goers to discover Hitchcock's timeless works.

TONY NOURMAND

CAHIERS DU CINEMA

ALFRED HITCHCOCK

Cahiers Du Cinema (1980)   Special edition featuring articles from previous publications on Hitchcock.

THE PLEASURE GARDEN (1925)

The 26-year-old Hitchcock made his directing debut with this romantic melodrama – an under-financed Anglo-German co-production made at the Emelka Studios in Munich and shot partly on location in Italy – which shows the influence of Griffith and Murnau. The plot, a backstage story of two chorus girls at the Pleasure Garden Theatre, contrasts the decent Virginia Valli, then a big star at Universal, with the coquettish Carmelita Geraghty. The idealistic Valli grows increasingly disillusioned after her marriage to a drunken rake (Miles Mander) who takes up with, and ultimately drowns, a native girl in a British colony in the Far East. Hitchcock would refashion the elements of this story – madness, murder and despair – to greater advantage in his subsequent films.

The Pleasure Garden /
Il Labirinto Delle Passioni (1925)
Emelka / Gainsborough
Italian 55 x 79 in. (140 x 201 cm)

The Pleasure Garden (1925)
Emelka / Gainsborough
US 41 x 27 in. (104 x 69 cm)

THE LODGER: A STORY OF THE LONDON FOG (1926)
US title: The Case Of Jonathan Drew

Nearly shelved by its distributor for being too dark and expressionistic, Hitchcock's technically innovative first suspense film starred England's leading matinee idol, Ivor Novello, as a man suspected of being a Jack the Ripper-like killer known as The Avenger. The mysterious muffled stranger prowls around at night carrying a black bag and murdering weekly as panic envelops the city. The theme of an innocent protagonist accused of a crime he has not committed was one of Hitchcock's favourites and would be recycled in a number of his movies, including **The 39 Steps**, **Young and Innocent**, **Saboteur**, **To Catch A Thief** and **North by Northwest**. Hitchcock appeared twice as an extra here; his cameos beginning with **Blackmail** later became his trademark. The visual experimentation, including a see-through ceiling, is noteworthy. A smash hit, the first true Hitchcock film was praised by the press as 'possibly the finest British production ever made'.

The French title refers to the fact that the culprit prefers to slay blondes. The imagery of the poster is suggestive of the crucifixion – the innocent Novello is suspended helplessly from a spiked railing, the scapegoat of an angry mob.

The Kinematograph Weekly
(27th May 1926)

The Lodger / Les Cheveux D'Or (1926)
Gainsborough
French 63 x 47 in. (160 x 119 cm)

DOWNHILL (1927)
US title: When Boys Leave Home

Co-written by Novello, this visually inventive tale concerns a youth who is unfairly expelled from school and banished by his stern father for allegedly impregnating a deceitful waitress. His social and spiritual downfall become increasingly pitiful once he is a gigolo living in squalor in Europe. Novello, who starred in the stage version, was, at 35, simply too old for the part.

The poster showing Novello descending a stairway (actually an escalator in an underground station) was a symbolic device of expressionistic directors Lang and Murnau.

Downhill / C'Est La Vie (1927)
Gainsborough
French 63 x 47 in. (160 x 119 cm)
Art by Pierre Pigeot

CHAMPAGNE (1928)

Spoiled and headstrong Betty Balfour gets a taste of the real world selling flowers in a cabaret after her Wall Street tycoon father pretends he is impoverished in order to prove that her boyfriend is a fortune hunter. Balfour was at the time Britain's leading female star.

Champagne / Palace De Luxe (1928)
British International
French 63 x 94 in. (160 x 239 cm)
Art by Venabert

Champagne / Palace De Luxe (1928)
British International
French 63 x 47 in. (160 x 119 cm)
Art by Venabert

MAPPEMONDE FILM PRÉSENTE

PALACE DE LUXE

AVEC BETTY BALFOUR

MARCEL VIBERT & JACK TRÉVOR

PRODUCTION
BRITISH INTERNATIONAL PICTURES

MAPPEMONDE FILM
28, Place St. Georges
PARIS

13

BLACKMAIL (1929)

Having starred in Hitchcock's previous film, **The Manxman** (1929), Polish-born Anny Ondra appears to have been the first in a succession of ice-cool blondes with whom Hitchcock became fascinated. The actress plays a tobacconist's daughter who becomes conscience-stricken after fatally stabbing a pickup artist (Cyril Ritchard) during an attempted seduction or rape? All the while Ondra's detective boyfriend (John Longden) conceals incriminating evidence: her glove, prefiguring the cigarette lighter in **Strangers On A Train.** Seemingly a simple story of love versus duty, **Blackmail** is actually memorably ironic and profound. Based on a hit play and begun as a silent, this became Britain's first synchronous-sound feature film. The landmark talkie is noted for its innovative sound and special effects, including a famous chase scene through the British Museum, culminating in the blackmailer's fall from the domed roof.

Future director Ronald Neame was the 'clapperboy' on the film; Michael Powell was the stills cameraman.

Blackmail (1929)
British International / Gainsborough
US Lobby Card: 11 x 14 in. (28 x 36 cm)

Blackmail (1929)
British International / Gainsborough
US Lobby Card: 11 x 14 in. (28 x 36 cm)

JUNO AND THE PAYCOCK (1930)

Set in the early 1920s during the Irish civil war, Hitchcock and Alma Reville's adaptation of Sean O'Casey's play depicts the hardships of a poor Dublin family.

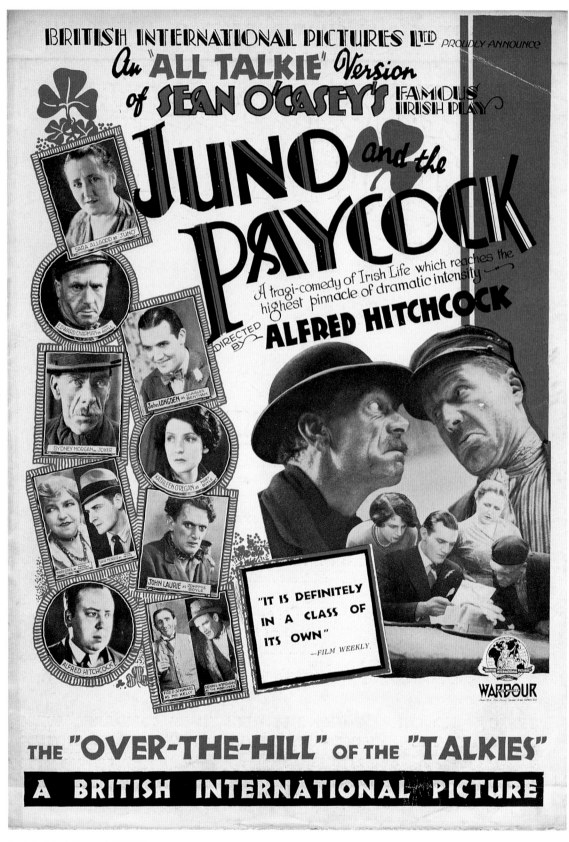

Juno And The Paycock (1930)
British International
16   British Pressbook Cover

WALTZES FROM VIENNA (1933)
US title: Strauss' Great Waltz
Johann Strauss junior (Esmond Knight), alienated from his illustrious musician father (Edmund Gwenn), struggles to compose the **Blue Danube** waltz while working in a bakery alongside leading lady Jessie Matthews (who was then Britain's top female star). Hitchcock was perhaps out of his element in this, his only musical, despite being again in the employ of his friend Michael Balcon, the production head at Gaumont-British.

Waltzes From Vienna / Le Chant Du Danube
(1933)
(US Title: **Strauss's Great Waltz**)
Gaumont-British
French 63 x 47 in. (160 x 119 cm)

THE MAN WHO KNEW TOO MUCH (1934)

An English couple on holiday (Leslie Banks and Edna Best) attempt to rescue their kidnapped daughter (Nova Pilbeam) and to foil the assassination of a foreign dignitary at The Royal Albert Hall. This characteristic suspense thriller – a big hit at the time – represents something of a comeback for Hitchcock (as **Strangers On A Train** would nearly two decades later). The first of the director's classic thriller sextet at Gaumont-British between 1934–38 is a more spontaneous, if less polished, version than his 1956 remake.

Peter Lorre, who achieved notoriety earlier as a child murderer in Fritz Lang's famed **M** (1931), makes for a superb angst-ridden anarchist in his first English-language film.

**The Man Who Knew Too Much/
I Manden Der Vidste For Meget** (1934)
Gaumont-British
Dutch 39 x 28 in. (99 x 71 cm)
Art by Crikf

The Man Who Knew Too Much (1934)
Gaumont-British
US 41 x 27 in. (104 x 69 cm)

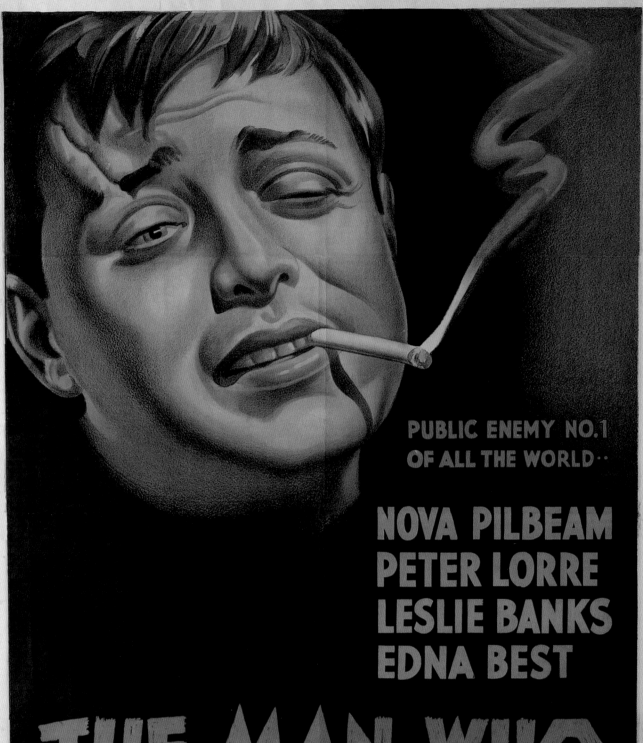

PUBLIC ENEMY NO.1
OF ALL THE WORLD··

**NOVA PILBEAM
PETER LORRE
LESLIE BANKS
EDNA BEST**

THE MAN WHO
KNEW TOO MUCH

A  PRODUCTION

Directed by ALFRED HITCHCOCK

THE 39 STEPS (1935)

A visiting Canadian (Robert Donat) comes under suspicion for murder; he flees to Scotland in an effort to explore a sinister spy network headed by Godfrey Tearle, who shows he is missing a fingertip in a memorable scene. Loosely based on John Buchan's 1915 novel and improved by screen-writing collaborator Charles Bennett, this deliberately disjointed and relentlessly paceful espionage thriller is generally considered the director's best 1930s picture. **The 39 Steps** was one of Hitchcock's favourite films, he thought that the tempo was perfect.

The film's famous sound edit combines a visual of the landlady's scream with the sound of a train whistle. Railway travel figures prominently in the action of the story (as it would in **The Lady Vanishes**, **Strangers On A Train** and **North by Northwest**). Despite the success of **The Man Who Knew Too Much**, distributor C.M. Woolf tried to cancel production on **The 39 Steps**.

The 39 Steps (1935)
Gaumont-British
US Lobby Card: 11 x 14 in. (28 x 36 cm)

The 39 Steps / 39 Stupno (1935)
Gaumont-British
Czech 38 x 12 in. (97 x 30 cm)

The 39 Steps (1935)
Gaumont-British
US 81 x 41 in. (206 x 104 cm)

SABOTAGE (1936)
US title: The Woman Alone

This adaptation of Joseph Conrad's grim novel **The Secret Agent** depicts Oscar Homolka as a cinema manager married to Sylvia Sidney. Tragedy strikes when Sidney's husband dupes her younger brother into carrying a bomb, which explodes, killing the brother. Sidney then takes her revenge by stabbing her husband.

The conspiratorial political intrigue was considered so subversive that the picture was banned in Brazil. Hitchcock was now the most famous British film-maker on both sides of the Atlantic.

Sabotage (1936)
(US Title: **The Woman Alone**)
Gaumont-British
US Lobby Card: 11 x 14 in. (28 x 36 cm)

Sabotage (1936)
(US Title: **The Woman Alone**)
Gaumont-British
US 81 x 41 in. (206 x 104 cm)

SECRET AGENT (1936)

Ashenden (John Gielgud), a character based on Somerset Maugham's spy stories, goes on an Alpine holiday hoping to unmask an enemy agent (Robert Young). Madeleine Carroll poses as Ashenden's wife and Peter Lorre plays a quirky trained assassin. **Secret Agent** is a disturbing spy tale set during World War One and designed to illustrate the danger of neutrality.

Secret Agent (1936)
Gaumont-British
US Lobby Card: 11 x 14 in. (28 x 36 cm)

Secret Agent (1936)
Gaumont-British
British Pressbook Cover

Secret Agent (1936)
Gaumont-British
US 41 x 27 in. (104 x 69 cm)

YOUNG AND INNOCENT (1937)
US title: The Girl Was Young

Former child star Nova Pilbeam – the kidnapping victim in **The Man Who Knew Too Much**, who was now 16 – reappears in this light-hearted and unpretentious mystery shot on location in Cornwall. Playing the daughter of a local constable, Pilbeam shelters a suspected murderer (Derrick De Marney) and a charming romance develops.

The highlight of this generally underrated film is a stunningly intricate crane shot of the twitching eyes of the guilt-ridden killer: a jazz drummer in blackface. It took two days to shoot and is one continuous move lasting one minute and ten seconds and focusing down from 145 feet to 4 inches.

Young And Innocent (1937)
(US Title: **The Girl Was Young**)
Gaumont-British
US Lobby Card: 11 x 14 in. (28 x 36 cm)

Young And Innocent (1937)
(US Title: **The Girl Was Young**)
Gaumont-British
US 41 x 27 in. (104 x 69 cm)

THE LADY VANISHES (1938)

On a transcontinental train journey through Central Europe, Margaret Lockwood and Michael Redgrave (in his film debut) strive to fathom the inexplicable disappearance of an elderly governess, Dame Mae Whitty. She is in fact a British agent trying to return to England with vital information encoded in the melody of a Balkan folk song. However her whereabouts are of no concern whatsoever to a couple of die-hard cricket enthusiasts anxious to return home in time for a big match. Despite its shoestring budget (a 90-feet-long set sufficed) and implausible plot, it is one of Hitchcock's most accomplished works.

For this, his biggest British money-maker, Hitchcock received the Best Director Award from the New York film critics.

The Lady Vanishes (1938)
Gainsborough/Gaumont-British
US Lobby Card: 11 x 14 in. (28 x 36 cm)

The Lady Vanishes (1938)
Gainsborough/Gaumont-British
US 36 x 14 in. (91 x 36 cm)

The Lady Vanishes (1938)
Gainsborough/Gaumont-British
US 41 x 27 in. (104 x 69 cm)

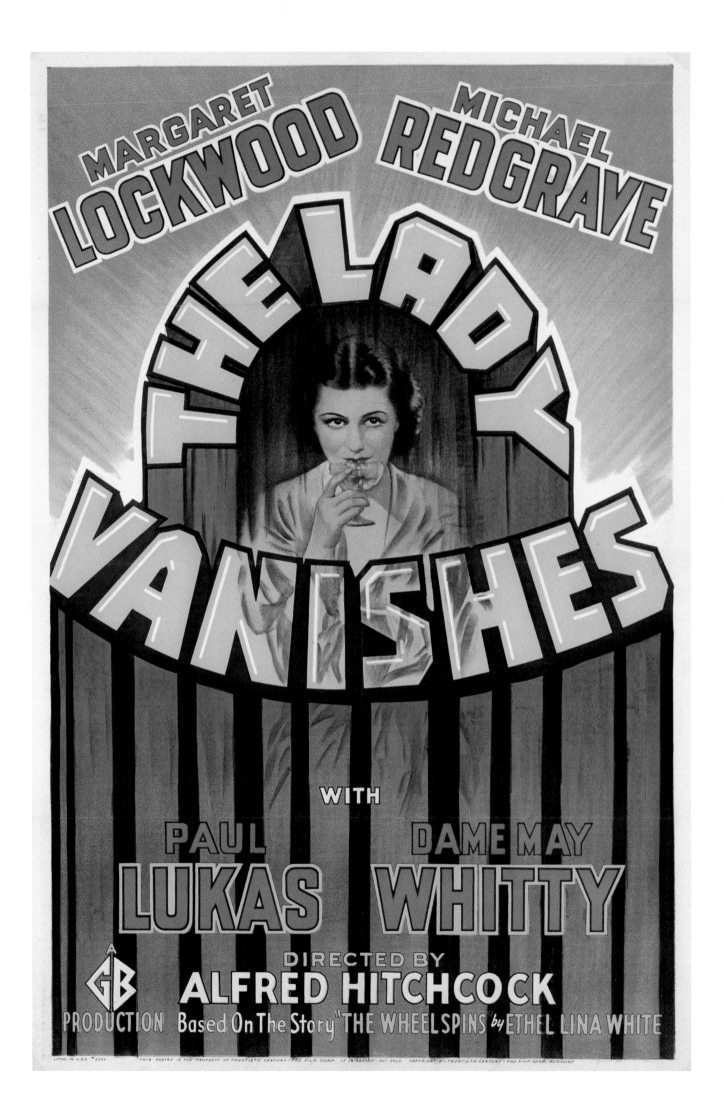

JAMAICA INN (1939)

The final pre-war film in Hitchcock's British period is a costume melodrama about a band of smugglers operating out of a remote Cornish Inn. Hitchcock was by now already bound for Hollywood, having signed a contract with David O. Selznick.

Jamaica Inn /
La Taverna Della Giamaica (1939)
Mayflower Pictures
Italian 79 x 55 in. (201 x 140 cm)
Art by C. Bompiani

Jamaica Inn (1939)
Mayflower Pictures
US 41 x 27 in. (104 x 69 cm)
(Style A)

FOREIGN CORRESPONDENT (1940)

As the title character, newspaperman Joel McCrea rescues a Dutch diplomat who has been abducted by the Nazis. In doing so, he is unaware that the chief Nazi is the apparently pacifist father of his love interest. Although Hitchcock may have been disappointed that Gary Cooper was unable to star in this chase thriller, the fast pace stands out as does Robert Benchley's droll wit and William Cameron Menzies' sets (such as the memorable Dutch windmill scene). The film was nominated for Best Picture (losing to **Rebecca**) and was intended to nudge US public opinion towards intervention in the war against Germany.

Foreign Correspondent (1940)
United Artists
US Lobby Card: 11 x 14 in. (28 x 36 cm)

**Foreign Correspondent /
Enviado Especial** (1940)
United Artists
Spanish 40 x 27 in. (102 x 69 cm)

REBECCA (1940)

A psychological drama adapted from Daphne du Maurier's bestseller, **Rebecca** transports us to Manderley, the ancestral home of tormented Maxim de Winter (Laurence Olivier) and his new bride (Joan Fontaine). What really happened to his faithless first wife, Rebecca, who remains a haunting presence throughout the picture? Although a seemingly English production, Hitchcock's American debut for Selznick was a superbly nuanced Gothic entertainment. This sure-fire crowd-pleaser won the Oscar for Best Picture; Hitchcock received his first (of five) nomination for Best Director.

According to Peter Bogdanovich, David O. Selznick wanted to add a touch of his own to the end of **Rebecca**. As the house is burning, he wanted the camera to pull back to show the smoke from the burning building forming the letter 'R' in the sky. Hitchcock's response: 'Can you imagine!'

Rebecca (1940)
Selznick International
US Lobby Card: 11 x 14 in. (28 x 36 cm)

Rebecca (1940)
Selznick International
US Herald

Rebecca (1940)
Selznick International
US 81 x 41 in. (206 x 104 cm)

MR AND MRS SMITH (1941)

A husband and wife, who have just discovered that their stormy marriage is void due to a minor technicality, live apart and begin courting anew. This screwball romantic comedy paired affable Robert Montgomery and beguiling Carole Lombard in her next-to-last picture before her fatal plane crash.

Mr And Mrs Smith (1941)
RKO
2 US Lobby Cards:
each 11 x 14 in. (28 x 36 cm)

Mr And Mrs Smith (1941)
RKO
US Rotogravure 41 x 27 in.
(104 x 69 cm)

The Riotous Intimate Comedy of a Bride Who Couldn't Stay MAD!

IN "MR. AND MRS. SMITH", Carole Lombard returns to the realm of high comedy she dominates so completely — and to the gorgeous smart clothes which long have made her one of the world's best-dressed women.

ROBERT MONTGOMERY and Carole busy at the serious business of creating laughs as they check with the Norman Krasna script between calls on the set.

UNDER-COVER GIRL Carole wonders what hubby Bob is going to do about it now that he has discovered that their marriage of three years is illegal.

OFF-STAGE ANTICS. Cut-up Carole presents Bob Montgomery with a piece of trick birthday cake, a little stunt hubby Clark Gable pulled on friend wife only the day before.

DIRECTOR ALFRED HITCHCOCK gets a laugh out of the stars and production staff as he puts the finishing touches on a comedy luncheon scene.

NEVER A DULL MOMENT as Carole and Bob try to run their merry marriage according to rules — never to leave their bedroom until they have patched up their latest quarrel. Looks like the exception that proves the rule here.

BOB FEIGNS ILLNESS as Carole gives him the once-over-lightly. If you ask us, he'd better snap out of it quick if he values his life!

A COUPLE OF LAW PARTNERS and an unlawful wife. Bob, Carole and Gene Raymond, who hopes to catch Carole on the bounce when she deserts her flippant, philandering husband. But a wild and woolly week-end at Lake Placid you'll not soon forget fixes all that.

CAROLE LOMBARD
ROBERT MONTGOMERY
in
Mr. & Mrs. Smith

with GENE RAYMOND
JACK CARSON · PHILIP MERIVALE · LUCILE WATSON
DIRECTED BY
ALFRED HITCHCOCK
HARRY E. EDINGTON—EXECUTIVE PRODUCER
STORY AND SCREEN PLAY BY NORMAN KRASNA

RKO RADIO PICTURES

DIRECTOR HITCHCOCK, who made "Rebecca" and "Foreign Correspondent", rehearses Carole and Bob for the close-shave scene shown above. Bob evidently objected to the hard floor. Note finished scene was shot in a comfortable bed.

PRINTED IN U.S.A.

SUSPICION (1941)

Joan Fontaine suspects that her handsome playboy husband (Cary Grant) is out to murder her for her money. He is indeed a gambler and embezzler, but is not quite as wicked as he seems. In the original ending, Grant poisons her, but Hitchcock was persuaded by the studio to change it for the sake of Grant's image. For her understated performance Fontaine received the Best Actress Academy Award.

Suspicion (1941)
RKO
US Lobby Card:
11 x 14 in. (28 x 36 cm)
(1953 Re-release)

Suspicion (1941)
RKO
US Lobby Card:
11 x 14 in. (28 x 36 cm)

38

Suspicion (1941)
RKO
US 81 x 41 in. (206 x 104 cm)

CARY JOAN
GRANT · **FONTAINE**
IN

Suspicion

with

SIR CEDRIC HARDWICKE
NIGEL BRUCE
DAME MAY WHITTY

Directed by
ALFRED HITCHCOCK

Screen play by Samson Raphaelson, Joan Harrison, Alma Reville

SABOTEUR (1942)

A Californian aircraft factory worker (Robert Cummings) attempts to clear himself after being unjustly accused of sabotage . The thriller, released after Pearl Harbor and the US entry into the war, features outstanding set pieces and makes use of famous national landmarks (Boulder Dam and the Statue of Liberty) as backdrops for the action – an idea that was to reach its high-point (in every sense) atop Mount Rushmore in **North by Northwest**.

Saboteur / Danger (1942)
Universal
Italian 18 x 26 in. (46 x 66 cm)
(1940s Re-release)

Saboteur (1942)
Universal
US Lobby Card:
40   11 x 14 in. (28 x 36 cm)

Saboteur (1942)
Universal
US 41 x 27 in. (104 x 69 cm)
(Style C)

SHADOW OF A DOUBT (1943)

The heroine (Teresa Wright) is devastated to discover that her beloved Uncle Charlie (Joseph Cotten) has been murdering wealthy widows prior to his visit to her storybook hometown. Uncle Charlie was Hitchcock's first fully fledged psychopath – the forerunner of Norman Bates. Hitchcock commented: 'Our evil and our good are getting closer together ... we've become so sophisticated, you can barely tell one from the other.'

Shadow Of A Doubt (1943)
Universal
US Lobby Card: 11 x 14 in. (28 x 36 cm)

**Shadow Of A Doubt /
L'Ombre D'Un Doute** (1943)
Universal
Belgian 16 x 11 in. (41 x 28 cm)

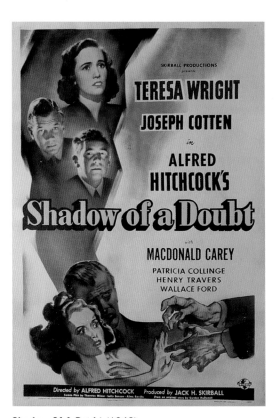

Shadow Of A Doubt (1943)
Universal
US 41 x 27 in. (104 x 69 cm)
(Style D)

Shadow Of A Doubt (1943)
Universal
US 81 x 41 in. (206 x 104 cm)
(Style A)

LIFEBOAT (1944)

The survivors from a torpedoed ship – a cross-section of humanity – try to coexist in a lifeboat in the Atlantic, guided by the skipper of the German sub that sank them. A stark single setting suffices for this drama which transfigures an original screen story by John Steinbeck.

Hitchcock initially signed with Selznick to direct a movie about the sinking of the **Titanic**, but the project never materialized. The director quipped 'I've had experience with icebergs. I directed Madeleine Carroll!'

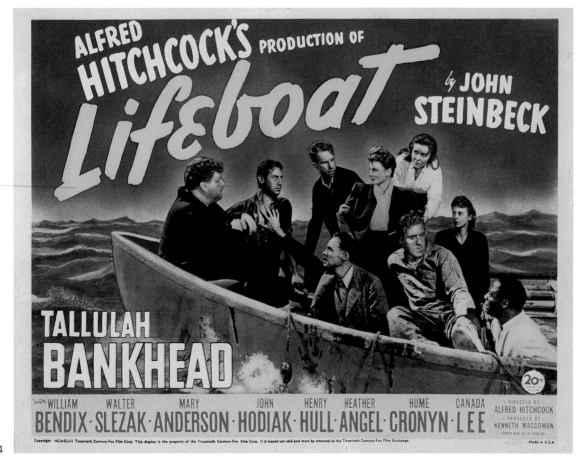

Lifeboat (1944)
20th Century Fox
US Lobby Card: 11 x 14 in. (28 x 36 cm)

Lifeboat (1944)
20th Century Fox
US 41 x 27 in. (104 x 69 cm)

SPELLBOUND (1945)

The new head of a mental asylum (Gregory Peck) may be a disturbed impostor, and an analyst (Ingrid Bergman) undertakes to resolve this psychoanalytical conundrum. While **Spellbound** was filmed in black and white, the gunshot momentarily turned the screen blood red. A surrealist dream sequence using Salvador Dali sets and the haunting, Oscar-winning Miklos Rozsa score are the highlights of this romantic melodrama.

Spellbound (1945)
Selznick International
US Lobby Card: 11 x 14 in. (28 x 36 cm)

Spellbound / Io Ti Salvero (1945)
Selznick International
Italian 79 x 55 in. (201 x 140 cm)
(1955 Re-release)
Art by Anselmo Ballester

Spellbound / Io Ti Salvero (1945)
Selznick International
Italian 55 x 39 in. (140 x 99 cm)
Art by Averardo Ciriello

Spellbound (1945)
Selznick International
US 24 Sheet
9 x 20 ft (2.75 x 6.9 m) (Part)

NOTORIOUS (1946)

Intelligence agent Cary Grant persuades his lover Ingrid Bergman, a traitor's daughter, to spy on Nazi sympathiser Claude Rains at close quarters – as his wife – and the alluring plaything is nearly poisoned as a consequence. Topical and perverse, this morally ambivalent chef d'oeuvre is set in Rio and makes the most of its perfect casting. This Selznick-originated vehicle was both produced and directed by Hitchcock for the first time in the US.

Notorious (1946)
RKO / Selznick International
US Lobby Card: 11 x 14 in. (28 x 36 cm)

Notorious / Les Enchaînés (1946)
RKO / Selznick International
French 31 x 24 in. (79 x 61 cm)
Art by Segogne

Notorious (1946)
RKO / Selznick International
US 81 x 41 in. (206 x 104 cm)

49

THE PARADINE CASE (1948)

When an enigmatic temptress, Mrs Paradine (Alida Valli), is put on trial for the murder of her blind older husband, her married defence lawyer (Gregory Peck) promptly falls in love with her. Hitchcock wanted Olivier and Garbo, not Peck and Valli, in this final Selznick release.

The Paradine Case (1948)
United Artists /
Selznick International
US Lobby Card:
11 x 14 in. (28 x 36 cm)

The Paradine Case (1948)
United Artists /
Selznick International
US 22 x 28 in. (56 x 71 cm)
(Style A)

The Paradine Case /
Le Procés Paradine (1948)
United Artists / Selznick International
Belgian 22 x 14 in. (56 x 36 cm)

Le Paris

Namur

Vendredi 7 - Samedi 8 -
Dimanche 9 Septembre
1962
ENFANTS NON ADMIS

CINÉ VOG FILMS S.A. PRÉSENTE

ALIDA VALLI

GREGORY PECK
ANN TODD
CHARLES LAUGHTON
CHARLES COBURN
ETHEL BARRYMORE
LOUIS JOURDAN

dans

UN FILM DE ALFRED HITCHCOCK

LE PROCÈS PARADINE
"THE PARADINE CASE"
HET PROCES PARADINE

SELZNICK STUDIO

ROPE (1948)

College philosophy professor James Stewart is aghast to discover that two of his students, John Dall and Farley Granger, emboldened by a mistaken sense of Nietzschean superiority, have just strangled a classmate. Having hidden the corpse in a chest in their penthouse apartment, they attend an elegant buffet dinner with the victim's fiancée and parents.

Hitchcock and James Stewart's first colour film was boldly experimental. It was shot with protracted 10-minute takes with the camera moving from room to room while unseen stage hands moved walls and furniture along the way. The director was eager to independently produce this continuous stage play based on the Leopold-Loeb murder case.

Rope / Cocktail Pour Un Cadavre (1948)
Transatlantic / Warner Brothers
Belgian 22 x 14 in. (56 x 36 cm)
(1950s Re-release)

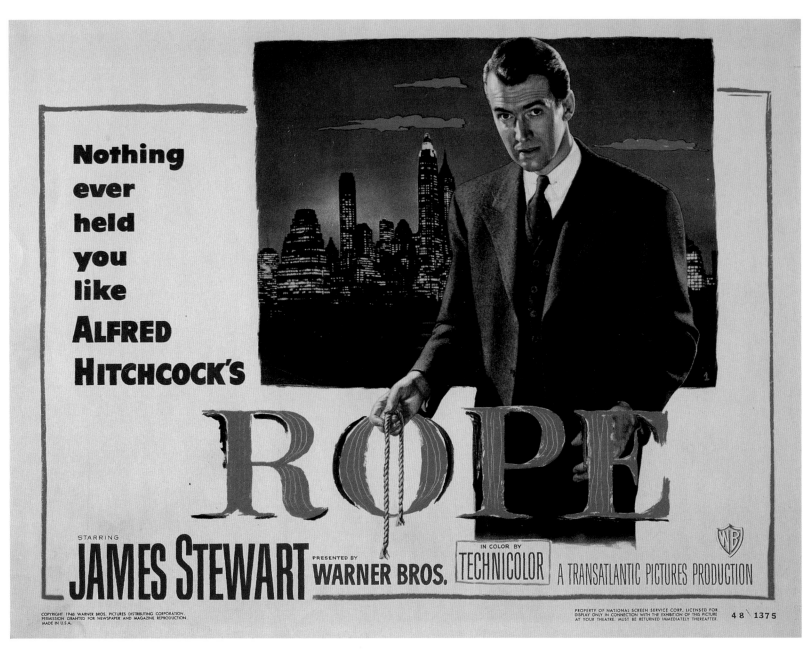

Rope (1948)
Transatlantic / Warner Brothers
US Lobby Card: 11 x 14 in. (28 x 36 cm)

UNDER CAPRICORN (1949)

Ingrid Bergman, an alcoholic aristocrat guilt-ridden over the death of her brother, shares a secret with her rich ex-con husband (Joseph Cotten). Set in Australia in the 1830s, this Brontësque costume drama, lushly photographed in Technicolor by Jack Cardiff, was unfortunately a flop despite the efforts of two of Hitchcock's favourite actors. The director wound up his production company, Transatlantic Pictures, as a result of the failure.

Under Capricorn (1949)
Sociedade Importadora De Filme
US Lobby Card: 11 x 14 in. (28 x 36 cm)

Under Capricorn /
Les Amants Du Capricorne (1949)
Sociedade Importadora De Filme
Belgian 22 x 14 in. (56 x 36 cm)

WARNER BROS présente

INGRID BERGMAN ★ JOSEPH COTTEN
MICHAEL WILDING

dans

COULEUR DE **Technicolor**

LES AMANTS DU CAPRICORNE

"UNDER CAPRICORN"

MISE EN SCÈNE **ALFRED HITCHCOCK**

SLAVIN VAN HAAR HART

STAGE FRIGHT (1950)

Richard Todd enlists the aid of actress friend Jane Wyman, a student at the Royal Academy of Dramatic Art, to exculpate himself from the murder of musical star Marlene Dietrich's husband. Wyman impersonates a cockney maid in her home, but Todd is ultimately unmasked as the culprit despite a misleading flashback which points the finger of blame at Dietrich.

Stage Fright (1950)
Warner Brothers
US Lobby Card: 11 x 14 in. (28 x 36 cm)

Stage Fright / Trema (1950)
Warner Brothers
Polish 33 x 23 in. (84 x 58 cm)
Art by Marek Frevdereich

MARLENA
DIETRICH W
SENSACYJNYM DRAMACIE
ALFREDA
HITCHCOCKA
TREMA
W
PO ZOSTAŁYCH
ROLACH
JANE
WYMAN MICHAEL WILDING
RICHARD TODD I INNI
PRODUKCJA WARNER BROS

STRANGERS ON A TRAIN (1951)

In the course of a chance meeting on a train, Robert Walker coolly offers to kill Farley Granger's estranged wife if the tennis star agrees to get rid of Walker's autocratic father. As there will be no evident motive for either of the 'criss-cross' slayings, they will not be suspected. Co-scripted by Raymond Chandler from Patricia Highsmith's novel, this masterfully cynical and compelling gem offers considerable food for thought. After all, Granger is legally an accessory after the fact. Rohmer and Chabrol elaborate on this transfer of guilt theory, first evidenced in **The Lodger**, in their trailblazing critical study **Hitchcock**. Although the director may have wanted William Holden for Granger's role, Robert Walker's finessed performance as the flamboyant psychopath is certainly inspired. The film's success re-established Hitchcock's stature as an independent producer and director.

This is the first of twelve films which Hitchcock made with cinematographer Robert Burks. In the first minute and fourteen seconds Hitchcock manages to convey the character of the two protagonists by focusing only on their shoes.

Strangers On A Train (1951)
Warner Brothers
British 30 x 40 in.
(76 x 102 cm)
(1950s Re-release)

Strangers On A Train (1951)
Warner Brothers
US Lobby Card:
11 x 14 in. (28 x 36 cm)

Strangers On A Train/Nieznajomi Z Pociagu
(1951)
Warner Brothers
Polish 33 x 23 in. (84 x 58 cm)
Art by Witold Janowski

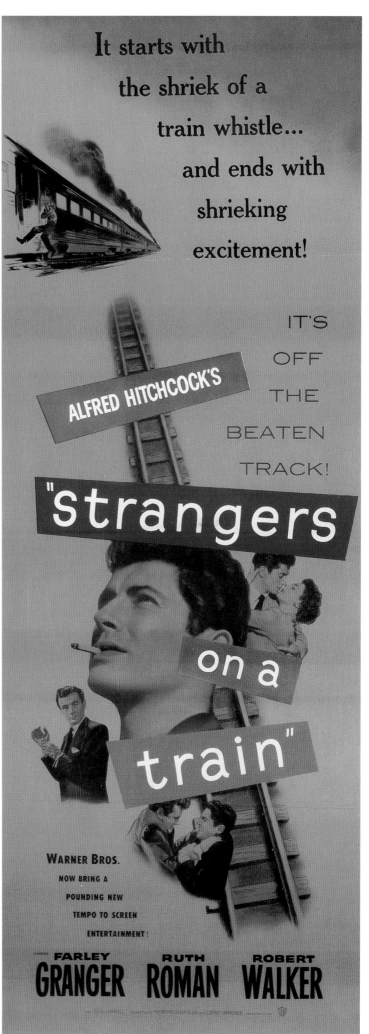

Strangers On A Train (1951)
Warner Brothers
US 36 x 14 in. (91 x 36 cm)

I CONFESS (1953)

A Canadian priest (Montgomery Clift) is compelled by his vows to shield a killer who has divulged his crime in the confessional. As the clergyman had a strong motive for the slaying, he is tried but is unable to defend himself. This slow paced, solemn film shot in Quebec reflects Hitchcock's strict Jesuit upbringing and represents an allegory of McCarthyism and the blacklist.

I Confess (1953)
Warner Brothers
US Lobby Card: 11 x 14 in. (28 x 36 cm)

I Confess / La Loi Du Silence (1953)
Warner Brothers
Belgian 22 x 14 in. (56 x 36 cm)

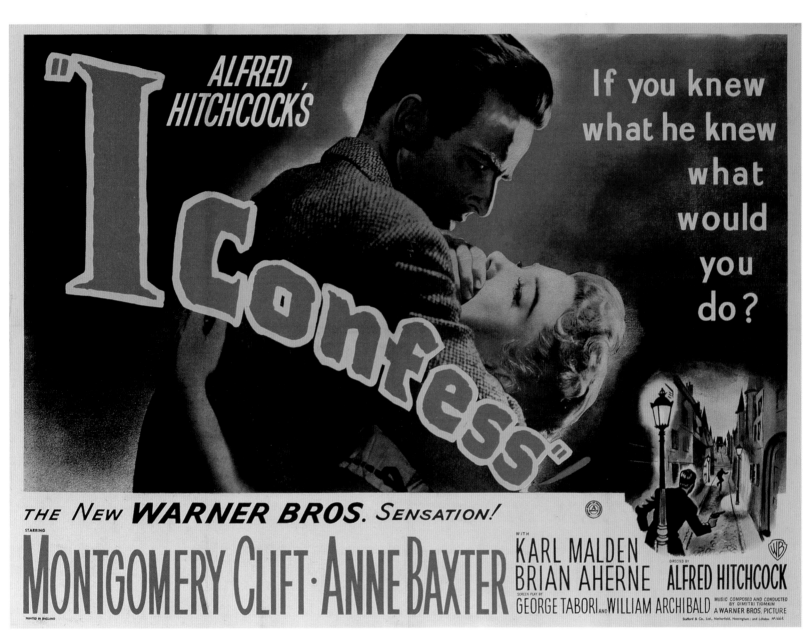

I Confess (1953)
Warner Brothers
British 30 x 40 in. (76 x 102 cm)

DIAL M FOR MURDER (1954)

A retired tennis champ (Ray Milland) decides to kill his wealthy wife (Grace Kelly) so she cannot ditch him for her writer lover (Robert Cummings). When Milland's accomplice is stabbed instead, Kelly is charged with – and nearly executed for – the crime. With most of the action taking place in one room, the cat-and-mouse dialogue and tidy plot stand out.

This was Hitchcock's fourteenth feature to be based on a (Broadway) play. It was filmed in 3-D, but released in a normal flat version.

Dial M For Murder (1954)
Warner Brothers
US Lobby Card: 11 x 14 in. (28 x 36 cm)

Dial M For Murder / Crimen Perfecto
(1954)
Warner Brothers
Spanish 40 x 27 in. (102 x 69 cm)
Art by Soligo

Dial M For Murder (1954)
Warner Brothers
British 30 x 40 in. (76 x 102 cm)

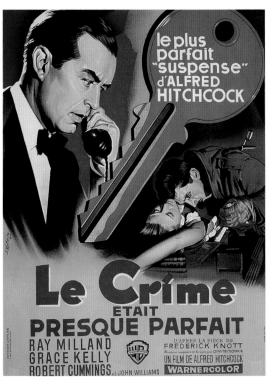

Dial M For Murder /
Le Crime Etait Presque Parfait (1954)
Warner Brothers
French 31 x 24 in. (79 x 61 cm)
(1958 Re-release)
Art by Joseph Koutachy

REAR WINDOW (1954)

Immobilized with a broken leg, a voyeuristic, misanthropic news photographer (James Stewart) passes the time spying on the neighbours across his Greenwich Village courtyard. But the Peeping Tom later has a hard time convincing others that a grisly murder has been committed. The acting is uniformly first rate. This timeless and flawless film was considered by Hitchcock to be his most 'cinematic' creation. With the camera never leaving the room, unless it is outside looking in, Hitchcock provocatively probed the relationship between the watcher and the watched, involving by extension the viewer of the film.

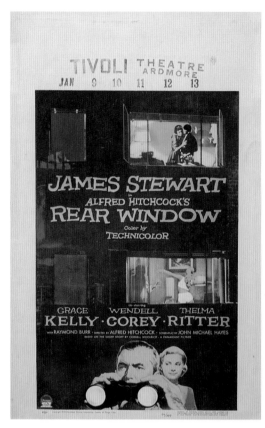

Rear Window (1954)
Paramount
US 22 x 14 in. (56 x 36 cm)

Rear Window / La Finestra Sul Cortile (1954)
Paramount
Italian 79 x 55 in. (201 x 140 cm)
Art by Averardo Ciriello

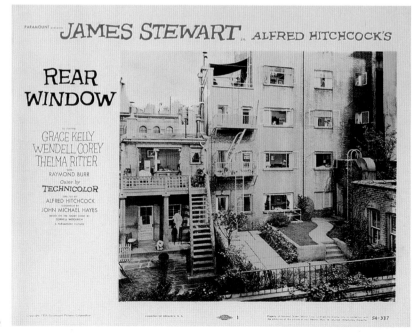

Rear Window (1954)
Paramount
US Lobby Card:
11 x 14 in. (28 x 36 cm)

Rear Window (1954)
Paramount
US 40 x 30 in. (102 x 76 cm)
(1962 Re-release)

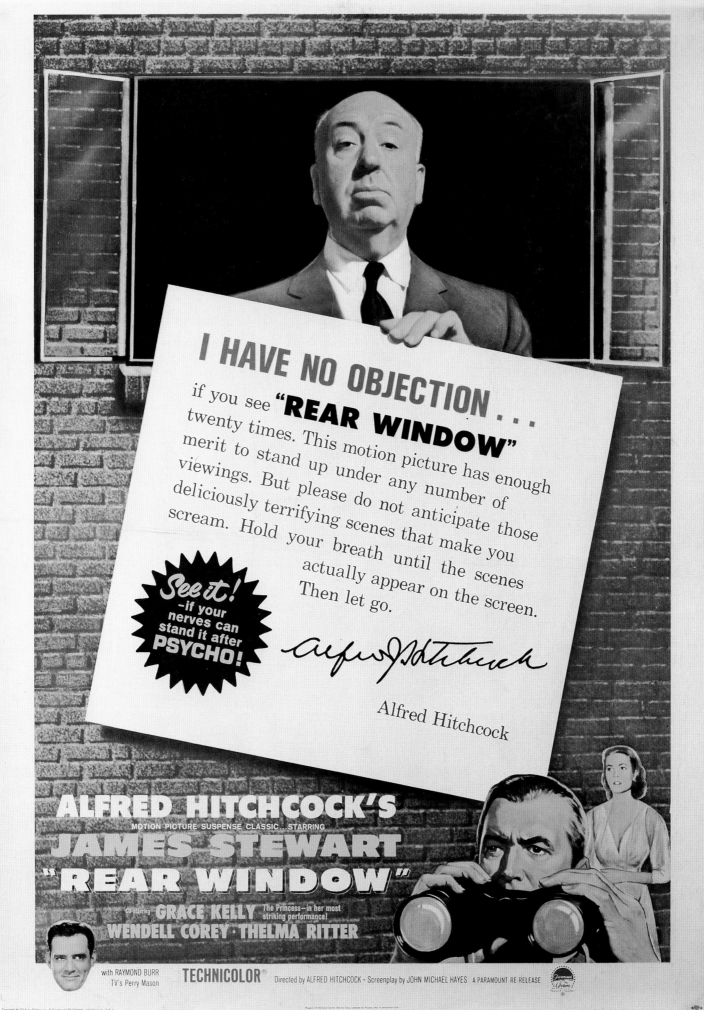

TO CATCH A THIEF (1955)

A suave one-time jewel thief known as 'Robie the Cat' (Cary Grant) is suspected of a series of robberies when a larcenous copycat begins using his **modus operandi** on the Cote d'Azur. Grant and Grace Kelly sparkle, as does the dazzling, scenic French Riviera. Robert Burks received an Academy Award for his Technicolor photography.

To Catch A Thief / Atrapa A Un Ladron (1955)
Paramount
Spanish Lobby Card: 11 x 14 in. (28 x 36 cm)

To Catch A Thief /
Caccia Al Ladro (1955)
Paramount
Italian 18 x 26 in. (46 x 66 cm)

To Catch A Thief / Caccia Al Ladro (1955)
Paramount
Italian 79 x 55 in. (201 x 140 cm)
Art by Ercole Brini

THE TROUBLE WITH HARRY (1955)

Who really killed Harry... and why does everyone keep burying and exhuming his corpse? This disarming, macabre black comedy was filmed in the autumnal Vermont countryside and gave Shirley MacLaine her film debut.

Bernard Herrmann composed the first of his eight scores for Hitchcock and cartoonist Charles Addams illustrated the credits.

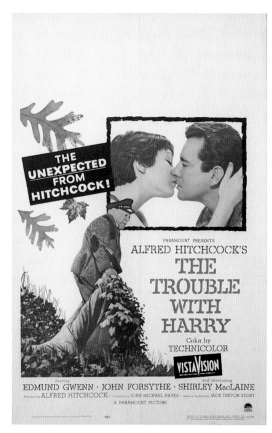

The Trouble With Harry (1955)
Paramount
US 22 x 14 in. (56 x 36 cm)

The Trouble With Harry /
Mais ... Qui A Tué Harry? (1955)
Paramount
Belgian 22 x 14 in. (56 x 36 cm)

The Trouble With Harry (1955)
Paramount
US Lobby Card:
68   11 x 14 in. (28 x 36 cm)

The Trouble With Harry (1955)
Paramount
Japanese 30 x 20 in. (76 x 51 cm)

名匠ヒッチコックが放つ
最高の話題作!!

VISTA VISION

MOTION PICTURE · HIGH FIDELITY

一つの屍体に四人の殺人ノイローゼ.
四人とも自分が犯人であるか、或は
その嫌疑をうける大きな理由をもっていた!!

ヒスタビジョン
総天然色

アルフレッド・ヒッチコック 製作監督
エドマンド・グエン
ジョン・フオーサイス
シャーリー・マクレーン
ミルドレッド・ナトウィック
ミルドレッド・ダノック

THE TROUBLE WITH HARRY

ハリーの災難
さいなん

69

THE MAN WHO KNEW TOO MUCH (1956)

In Hitchcock's only remake – it was filmed previously at Gaumont-British in 1934 – a distraught American tourist couple in Marrakesh (James Stewart and Doris Day) try to rescue their young son from kidnappers intent on assassinating a statesman. This considerably longer and more expansive version benefits from a more accessible plot, ampler characterization, widescreen VistaVision and Technicolor. Doris Day's rendition of the song **Que Sera Sera** won an Oscar.

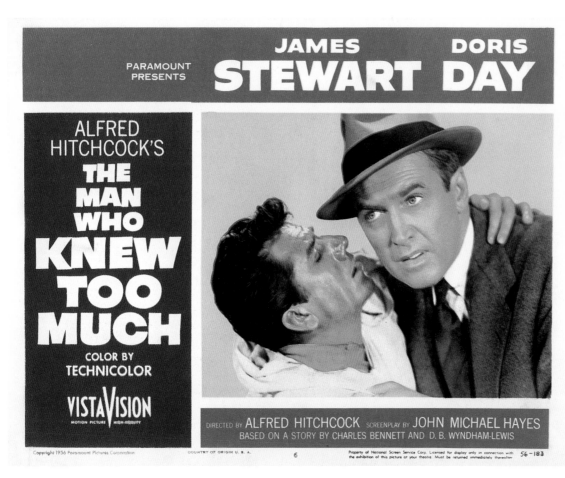

The Man Who Knew Too Much (1956)
Paramount
US Lobby Card: 11 x 14 in. (28 x 36 cm)

The Man Who Knew Too Much (1956)
Paramount
Japanese 30 x 20 in. (76 x 51 cm)

**The Man Who Knew Too Much /
L'Uomo Che Sapeva Troppo** (1956)
Paramount
Italian 79 x 55 in. (201 x 140 cm)
Art by Ercole Brini

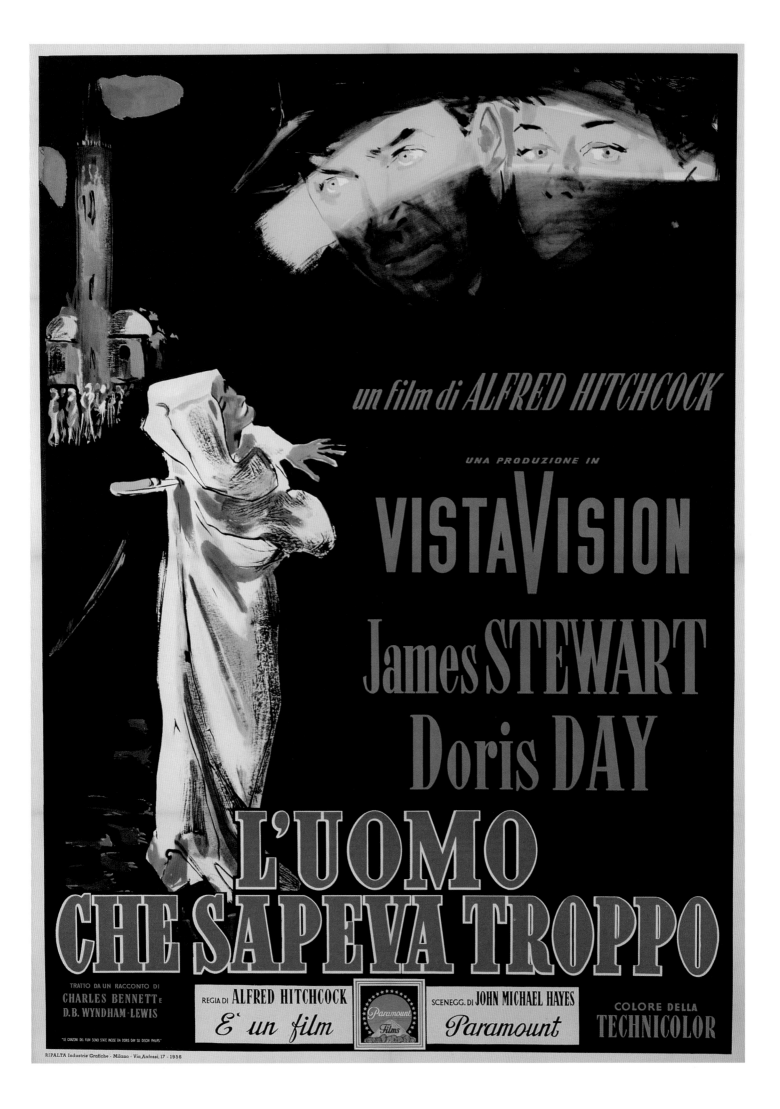

THE WRONG MAN (1957)

An innocent victim of circumstantial evidence, honest, hard-working musician Henry Fonda finds himself incriminated in a hold-up committed by his double, and the subsequent strain is such that his wife Vera Miles winds up in a mental institution. This black-and-white semi-documentary critique of the American justice system may have been too visually stark and austere for viewers. In addition, there is a sense of dislocation as the point of view shifts midway through the narrative from Fonda's misfortune to Miles' harrowing dramatics.

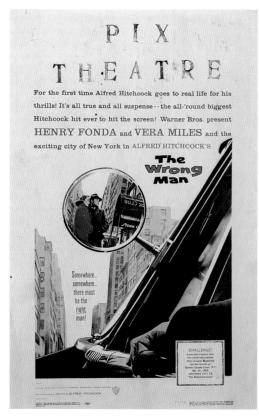

The Wrong Man (1957)
Warner Brothers
US 22 x 14 in. (56 x 36 cm)

The Wrong Man / Il Ladro (1957)
Warner Brothers
Italian 26 x 18 in. (66 x 46 cm)

The Wrong Man (1957)
Warner Brothers
US Lobby Card:
11 x 14 in. (28 x 36 cm)

The Wrong Man / Il Ladro (1957)
Warner Brothers
Italian 26 x 18 in. (66 x 46 cm)

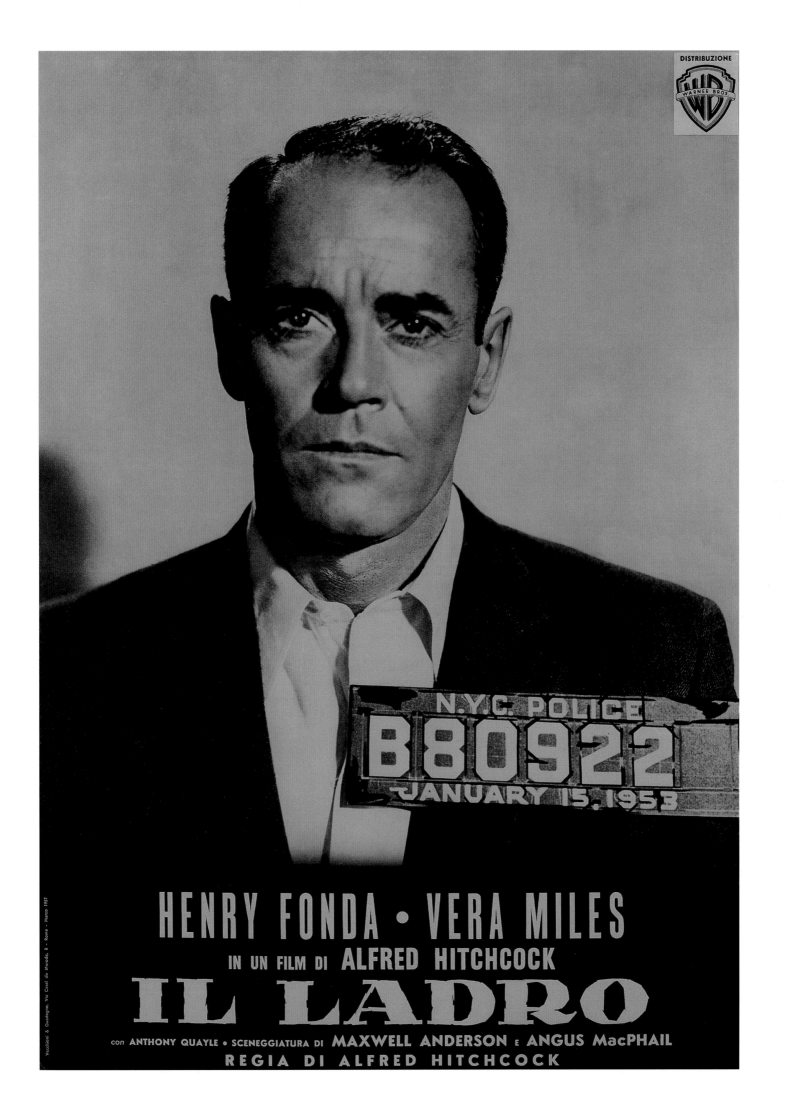

VERTIGO (1958)

Having resigned from the San Francisco police force, acrophobic James Stewart is hired to ensure the safety of the suicidal Madeleine (Kim Novak), an ethereal beauty who believes she is the reincarnation of her great-grandmother. The ex-detective, rendered helpless by vertigo, cannot save her when she jumps to her death from the bell tower of an old Spanish mission. Stewart falls to pieces before spotting her rather common look-alike, Judy, whom he proceeds to transform into his beloved Madeleine. Many consider this hypnotic, dizzying romantic fantasy Hitchcock's **chef d'oeuvre** because of both the subject matter – the yearning for an unattainable ideal – and its execution – the mesmerising beauty of Technicolor intensifying the hallucinatory and nightmarish mood.

Noted graphic artist Saul Bass (1920–96) designed the credit titles as well as the American film poster. Bass' spiral imagery represents Stewart's guilt on the staircase of the mission and is also a sexual metaphor. Hitchcock: 'Isn't it a fascinating design? One could study it for ever'.

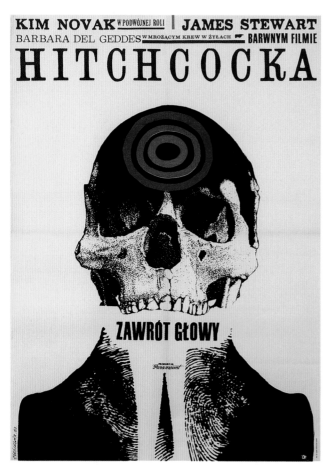

Vertigo / Zawrot Glowy (1958)
Paramount
Polish 33 x 23 in. (84 x 58 cm)
Art by Roman Cieslewicz

Vertigo / La Donna Che Visse Due Volte (1958)
Paramount
Italian 28 x 13 in. (71 x 33 cm)

Vertigo (1958)
Paramount
Japanese 30 x 20 in. (76 x 51 cm)

Vertigo (1958)
Paramount
US 40 x 30 in. (102 x 76 cm)

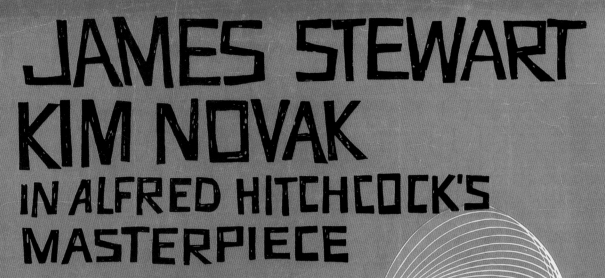

JAMES STEWART
KIM NOVAK
IN ALFRED HITCHCOCK'S
MASTERPIECE

'VERTIGO'

CO-STARRING
BARBARA BEL GEDDES WITH TOM HELMORE · HENRY JONES · DIRECTED BY ALFRED HITCHCOCK · SCREENPLAY BY ALEC COPPEL & SAMUEL TAYLOR · TECHNICOLOR®
BASED UPON THE NOVEL 'D'ENTRE LES MORTS' BY PIERRE BOILEAU AND THOMAS NARCEJAC · MUSIC BY BERNARD HERRMANN

VistaVision
MOTION PICTURE HIGH FIDELITY

Vertigo (1958)
Paramount
US Lobby Card: 11 x 14 in. (28 x 36 cm)

77

NORTH BY NORTHWEST (1959)

In this panoramic and resplendent final variation on the theme of **The 39 Steps**, advertising executive Cary Grant eludes spies, romances Eva Marie Saint and risks his neck throughout. A scintillating Ernest Lehman script was the catalyst for this seamless comedy thriller which the director considered the summit of his American output. Expertly chiselled, the film remains popular to the present day. According to Lehman, it is 'the Hitchcock picture to end all Hitchcock pictures. Hitch thought a good title might be 'The Man In Lincoln's Nose'. He loved that idea.'

North By Northwest (1959)
MGM
US 22 x 14 in. (56 x 36 cm)

North By Northwest (1959)
MGM
US 22 x 14 in. (56 x 36 cm)
(1966 Re-release)

North By Northwest (1959)
MGM
US Lobby Card:
11 x 14 in. (28 x 36 cm)

North By Northwest (1959)
MGM
Japanese 30 x 20 in. (76 x 51 cm)

NORTH BY NORTHWEST

PSYCHO (1960)

A supreme shocker then, and equally chilling today, **Psycho** was Hitchcock's biggest-grossing film. The surprise blockbuster, filmed economically on the Universal backlot, in part by his TV series crew, checks us into the infamous Bates Motel. The deranged, sexually repressed taxidermist proprietor (Anthony Perkins) repeatedly stabs a larcenous secretary (Janet Leigh) in a spellbindingly grisly shower scene. As Norman Bates – the shy, sensitive psychotic with a split personality and an Oedipus complex – Perkins has never been better. A horror film **par excellence** which Hitchcock deemed a 'fun' picture: a 'black comedy'. Although some critics labelled it too violent when it opened – it was 'a blot on an honourable career' according to **The New York Times** – there are actually more deaths in **Vertigo**.

Psycho (1960)
Paramount / Universal
US Lobby Card: 11 x 14 in. (28 x 36 cm)

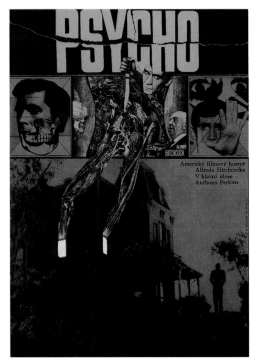

Psycho (1960)
Paramount / Universal
Czech 33 x 23 in. (84 x 58 cm)
Art by Z. Ziegler

Psycho (1960)
Paramount / Universal
US 81 x 41 in. (206 x 104 cm)

THE BIRDS (1963)

The Birds was made three years after Hitchcock filmed the last flickering image of the stuffed birds on the wall in the Bates Motel. He surmounted great technical challenges filming this disturbingly apocalyptic parable, based on the Daphne du Maurier story. Working in the sleepy community of Bodega Bay, a small fishing village north of San Francisco, Hitchcock's crew shot over 370 trick shots using both trained and fake birds. Hitchcock's deadpan ex-model protégée Tippi Hedren, making her film debut as a spoiled socialite, has to endure a pecking ordeal in an attic in a scene rendered terrifying thanks to Ub Iwerks' animation special effects.

Is the motiveless menace supposed to denote our helplessness – our sense of precariousness – or does it symbolize nature taking revenge?

The Birds (1963)
Universal
US Lobby Card: 11 x 14 in. (28 x 36 cm)

The Birds (1963)
Universal
US 41 x 27 in. (104 x 69 cm)

The Birds / Ptaki (1963)
Universal
Polish 33 x 23 in. (84 x 58 cm)
Art by Bronislaw Zelek

niesamowity film
ALFREDA HITCHCOCKA
wykonawcy: Rod Taylor
„Tippi"Hedren, JessicaTandy
Suzanne Pleshette
produkcja: Hitchcock-Universal

MARNIE (1964)

An inhibited, predatory equestrienne who is compelled to rob safes (Tipi Hedren) gets her comeuppance from widowed publisher, Sean Connery, an amateur psychoanalyst. The story line resembles the theme of **Spellbound**. Once again relating crime to violence and sex, Hitchcock claimed, 'We are all perverted in different ways.'

Marnie (1964)
Universal
US Lobby Card: 11 x 14 in. (28 x 36 cm)

Marnie (1964)
Universal
US 22 x 14 in. (56 x 36 cm)

Marnie (1964)
Universal
Italian 79 x 55 in. (201 x 140 cm)

ALFRED HITCHCOCK

Chi é MARNIE?

Una ladra?
Una bugiarda?
Una truffatrice?
Una sensuale?
Una adescatrice?
Sì,
e molto di più!

Vietato ai minori di 14 anni

MARNIE

con 'TIPPI' HEDREN · SEAN CONNERY

E DIANE BAKER · MARTIN GABEL   scenegg. JAY PRESSON ALLEN

DISTRIBUZIONE Universal International

TECHNICOLOR®

DAL ROMANZO DI WINSTON GRAHAM PUBBLICATO IN ITALIA DALLE 'EDIZIONI CASINI'   REGIA: ALFRED HITCHCOCK

TORN CURTAIN (1966)

Nuclear physicist Paul Newman fakes his defection to the Communist bloc for the sake of a secret scientific formula. A drawn out murder scene between the protagonist and a Communist agent leaves the viewer with a sense of moral discomfort.

When in Southern California visit Universal City Studios

PAUL JULIE
NEWMAN ANDREWS
in "ALFRED HITCHCOCK'S
'TORN CURTAIN'

co-starring LILA KEDROVA · HANSJOERG FELMY · TAMARA TOUMANOVA
LUDWIG DONATH · DAVID OPATOSHU · Music by JOHN ADDISON · Written by BRIAN MOORE
Directed by ALFRED HITCHCOCK · A Universal Picture **TECHNICOLOR**®

Copyright © 1966 by Universal Pictures Co., Inc. Country of Origin U.S.A. Printed in U.S.A.   3   Property of National Screen Service Corp. Licensed for display only in connection with the exhibition of this picture at your theatre. Must be returned immediately thereafter.   66/259

Torn Curtain (1966)
Universal
US Lobby Card: 11 x 14 in. (28 x 36 cm)

Torn Curtain (1966)
Universal
US 22 x 14 in. (56 x 36 cm)

PAUL JULIE
NEWMAN ANDREWS

ALFRED
HITCHCOCK'S
'TORN
CURTAIN' TECHNICOLOR.

IT
TEARS
YOU APART
WITH
SUSPENSE!

co-starring
LILA KEDROVA · HANSJOERG FELMY · TAMARA TOUMANOVA
LUDWIG DONATH · DAVID OPATOSHU · Music by JOHN ADDISON · Written by BRIAN MOORE
Directed by ALFRED HITCHCOCK · A Universal Picture

66/259

TOPAZ (1969)

A French counterspy (Frederick Stafford) helps the US ascertain the existence of a Soviet spy ring, code-named 'Topaz', which has infiltrated NATO besides verifying the proliferation of missile bases in Cuba.

Topaz (1969)
Universal
US Lobby Card: 11 x 14 in. (28 x 36 cm)

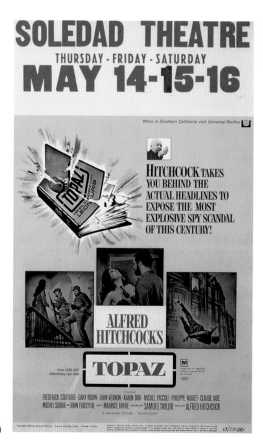

Topaz (1969)
Universal
US 22 x 14 in. (56 x 36 cm)

Topaz (1969)
Universal
Belgian 22 x 14 in. (56 x 36 cm)

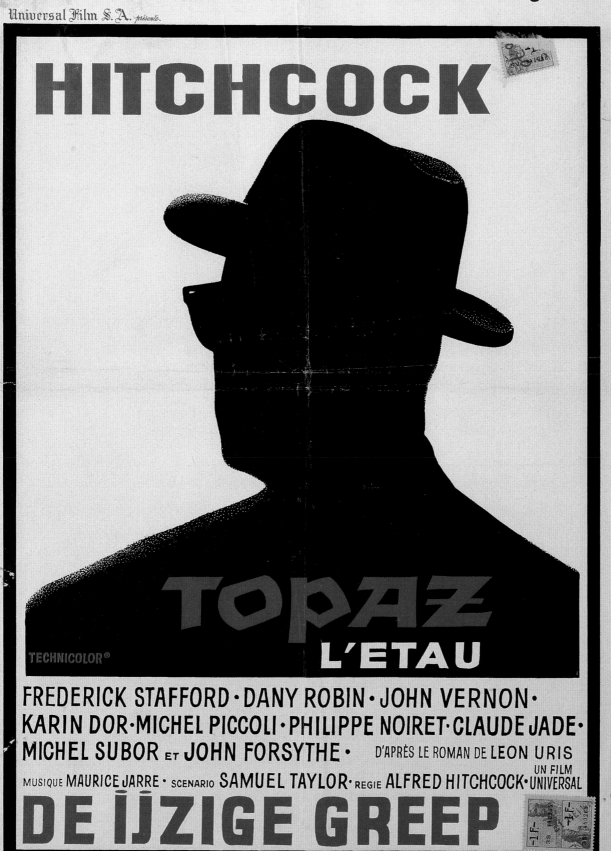

FRENZY (1972)

Frenzy marks Hitchcock's fortuitous return to England after 22 years. The thematic terrain is familiar – a sadistic killer is terrorizing London – in this riveting production which makes the most of its cast of unknowns. Protagonist Jon Finch, an unemployed bartender and former RAF squadron leader who is now down on his luck, has to lay low to clear himself from a rash of rape strangulations committed by 'The Necktie Killer', who is actually his cockney friend Barry Foster. His misplaced stickpin brings to mind Farley Granger's cigarette lighter in **Stranger's On A Train**.

Screenwriter Anthony Shaffer (**Sleuth**) collaborated splendidly with Hitchcock, creating not only repellent characters but also unforgettable comic relief.

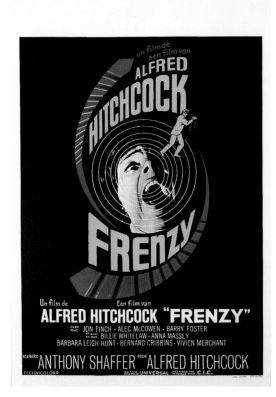

Frenzy (1972)
Universal
US 22 x 14 in. (56 x 36 cm)

Frenzy / Szal (1972)
Universal
Polish 33 x 23 in. (84 x 58 cm)
Art by Jan Mlodozeniec

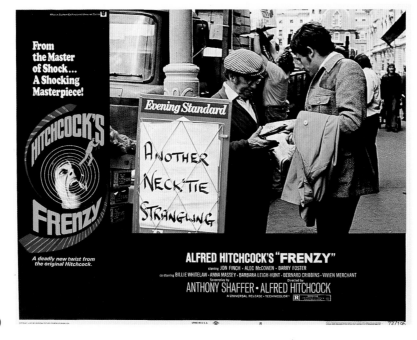

Frenzy (1972)
Universal
US Lobby Card:
11 x 14 in. (28 x 36 cm)

Frenzy / Frenesi (1972)
Universal
Spanish 13^1/$_2$ x 9^1/$_2$ in. (34 x 24 cm)

FAMILY PLOT (1976)

Ernest Lehman's parallel plots involve two different sets of characters whose paths keep crossing. A wealthy dowager enlists the services of a phoney medium (Barbara Harris) and her taxi-driver boyfriend (Bruce Dern) to locate her long-lost illegitimate nephew. The heir proves to be a kidnapper (William Devane) who is currently scheming to abduct the Bishop of San Francisco in the middle of mass with the aid of his accomplice (Karen Black). Ironically, the heir prefers the ransom money to the inheritance. Cleverly conceived, with tongue-in-cheek tomfoolery, this was a fitting finale to Hitchcock's prolific career.

Family Plot (1976)
Universal
US Lobby Card: 11 x 14 in. (28 x 36 cm)

Family Plot (1976)
Universal
Japanese 30 x 20 in. (76 x 51 cm)

EDWARD
SHOEBRIDGE
1933-1950

何かが追いかけてく
蜘蛛の糸にからまっ
2組の男女を

スリラーの巨匠、ヒッチコック
待望のサスペンス最新作!!

カレン・ブラック／ブルース・ダーン
バーバラ・ハリス／ウイリアム・ディベイン
キャスリン・ネスビット エド・ローター キャサリン・ヘルモント
監督 アルフレッド・ヒッチコック／脚本 アーネスト・リーマン／原作 ビクター・カニング「The Rainbird Pattern」より
撮影 レオナード・J・サウス／音楽 ジョン・ウイリアムス／衣装 エディス・ヘッド
〈カラー作品〉ユニヴァーサル映画 CIC配給

ヒッチコック映画製作50年記念作品
ヒッチコックの
ファミリー・
プロット

¡ALFRED HITCHCOCK'S FAMILY PLOT

[映倫]

WOMAN TO WOMAN (1923)

During World War One an English officer has an affair with a French girl, a dancer at the Moulin Rouge, who bears his child. After becoming an amnesiac due to a war wound, he returns to England and marries another woman. A **Random Harvest**-like denouement ensues.

Hitchcock was assistant director and art director for Graham Cutts – who was then the most successful director in England. The jack-of-all-trades, who was then sporting a Chaplinesque moustache, impressed script girl and editor Alma Reville whom he married three years later (12 February, 1926). The two worked side by side for the next half-century, with Alma serving as his literary collaborator and 'severest critic'. This film was an auspicious start for Hitchcock as it was quite profitable.

Woman To Woman (1923)
Wardor & F.
US 22 x 14 in. (56 x 36 cm)

The 39 Steps (1935)
Gaumont-British
Set of 8 US Lobby Cards: each 11 x 14 in. (28 x 36 cm)

Sabotage (1936)
(US Title: **The Woman Alone**)
Gaumont-British
Set of 8 US Lobby Cards:
each 11 x 14 in. (28 x 36 cm)

Secret Agent (1936)
Gaumont-British
Set of 8 US Lobby Cards:
each 11 x 14 in. (28 x 36 cm)

Young And Innocent (1937)
(US Title: **The Girl Was Young**)
Gaumont-British
Set of 8 US Lobby Cards:
each 11 x 14 in. (28 x 36 cm)

The Lady Vanishes (1938)
Gainsborough / Gaumont-British
Set of 8 US Lobby Cards:
each 11 x 14 in. (28 x 36 cm)

Jamaica Inn (1939)
Mayflower Pictures
Set of 8 British Lobby Cards:
each 11 x 14 in. (28 x 36 cm)

Jamaica Inn (1939)
Mayflower Pictures
Set of 8 US Lobby Cards:
each 11 x 14 in. (28 x 36 cm)

Jamaica Inn (1939)
Mayflower Pictures
Set of 8 US Lobby Cards:
each 11 x 14 in. (28 x 36 cm)
(Re-release)

Foreign Correspondent (1940)
United Artists
Set of 8 US Lobby Cards:
each 11 x 14 in. (28 x 36 cm)

Rebecca (1940)
Selznick International
Set of 8 US Lobby Cards:
each 11 x 14 in. (28 x 36 cm)

Mr And Mrs Smith (1941)
RKO
Set of 8 US Lobby Cards:
each 11 x 14 in. (28 x 36 cm)

Suspicion (1941)
RKO
Set of 8 US Lobby Cards:
each 11 x 14 in. (28 x 36 cm)

Saboteur (1942)
Universal
Set of 8 US Lobby Cards:
each 11 x 14 in. (28 x 36 cm)

Shadow Of A Doubt (1943)
Universal
Set of 8 US Lobby Cards:
each 11 x 14 in. (28 x 36 cm)

Lifeboat (1944)
20th Century Fox
Set of 8 US Lobby Cards:
each 11 x 14 in. (28 x 36 cm)

Spellbound (1945)
Selznick International
Set of 8 US Lobby Cards:
each 11 x 14 in. (28 x 36 cm)

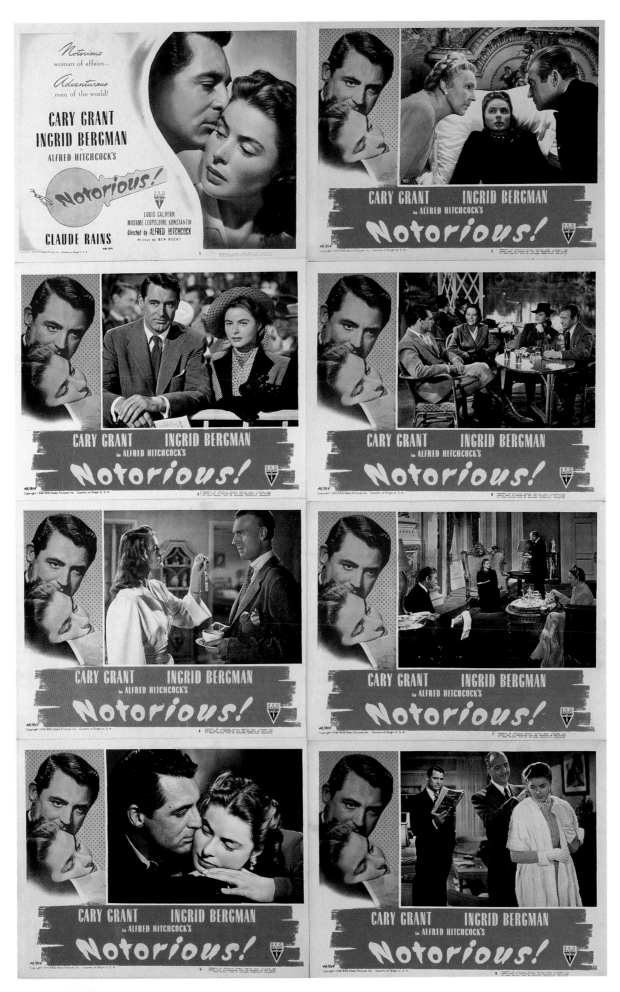

Notorious (1946)
RKO / Selznick International
Set of 8 US Lobby Cards:
each 11 x 14 in. (28 x 36 cm)

The Paradine Case (1948)
United Artists / Selznick International
Set of 8 US Lobby Cards:
each 11 x 14 in. (28 x 36 cm)

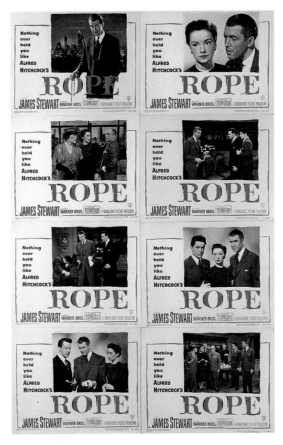

Rope (1948)
Transatlantic / Warner Brothers
Set of 8 US Lobby Cards:
each 11 x 14 in. (28 x 36 cm)

Under Capricorn (1949)
Sociedade Importadora De Filme
Set of 8 US Lobby Cards:
each 11 x 14 in. (28 x 36 cm)

Stage Fright (1950)
Warner Brothers
Set of 8 US Lobby Cards:
each 11 x 14 in. (28 x 36 cm)

Strangers On A Train (1951)
Warner Brothers
Set of 8 US Lobby Cards:
each 11 x 14 in. (28 x 36 cm)

I Confess (1953)
Warner Brothers
Set of 8 US Lobby Cards:
each 11 x 14 in. (28 x 36 cm)

Dial M For Murder (1954)
Warner Brothers
Set of 8 US Lobby Cards:
each 11 x 14 in. (28 x 36 cm)

Rear Window (1954)
Paramount
Set of 8 US Lobby Cards:
each 11 x 14 in. (28 x 36 cm)

Rear Window (1954)
Paramount
Set of 8 US Lobby Cards:
each 11 x 14 in. (28 x 36 cm)
(1962 Re-release)

To Catch A Thief (1955)
Paramount
Set of 8 US Lobby Cards:
each 11 x 14 in. (28 x 36 cm)

The Trouble With Harry (1955)
Paramount
Set of 8 US Lobby Cards:
each 11 x 14 in. (28 x 36 cm)

The Man Who Knew Too Much (1956)
Paramount
Set of 8 US Lobby Cards:
each 11 x 14 in. (28 x 36 cm)

The Wrong Man (1957)
Warner Brothers
Set of 8 US Lobby Cards:
each 11 x 14 in. (28 x 36 cm)

Vertigo (1958)
Paramount
Set of 8 US Lobby Cards:
each 11 x 14 in. (28 x 36 cm)

North By Northwest (1959)
MGM
Set of 8 US Lobby Cards:
each 11 x 14 in. (28 x 36 cm)

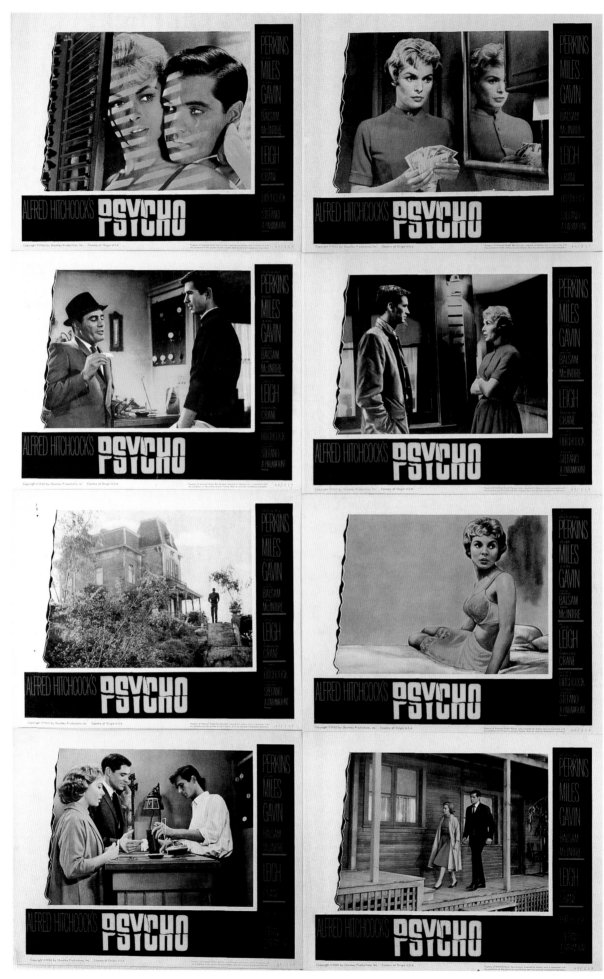

Psycho (1960)
Paramount / Universal
Set of 8 US Lobby Cards:
each 11 x 14 in. (28 x 36 cm)

The Birds (1963)
Universal
Set of 8 US Lobby Cards:
each 11 x 14 in. (28 x 36 cm)

Marnie (1964)
Universal
Set of 8 US Lobby Cards:
each 11 x 14 in. (28 x 36 cm)

Torn Curtain (1966)
Universal
Set of 8 US Lobby Cards:
each 11 x 14 in. (28 x 36 cm)

Topaz (1969)
Universal
Set of 8 US Lobby Cards:
each 11 x 14 in. (28 x 36 cm)
(No. 2)

Topaz (1969)
Universal
Set of 8 US Lobby Cards:
each 11 x 14 in. (28 x 36 cm)

Frenzy (1972)
Universal
Set of 8 US Lobby Cards:
each 11 x 14 in. (28 x 36 cm)

Family Plot (1976)
Universal
Set of 8 US Lobby Cards:
each 11 x 14 in. (28 x 36 cm)

Group of Homage Lobby Cards.

Group of Homage Lobby Cards.

Movie Tie-In Books for various Hitchcock films.

'TV Guide' (30th November 1957).
Illustration by Albert Hirschfeld.

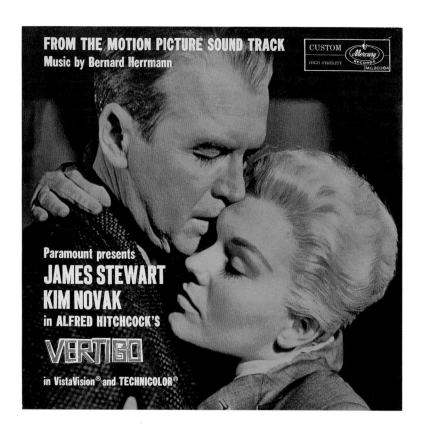

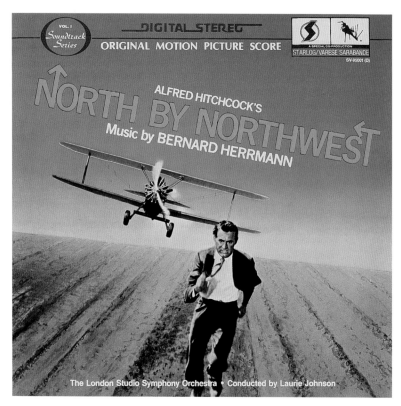

Two Record Album Covers featuring Bernard Herrmann
Soundtracks to **Vertigo** and **North By Northwest**.

'Music To Be Murdered By' (c. 1960s).
Record Album Cover.

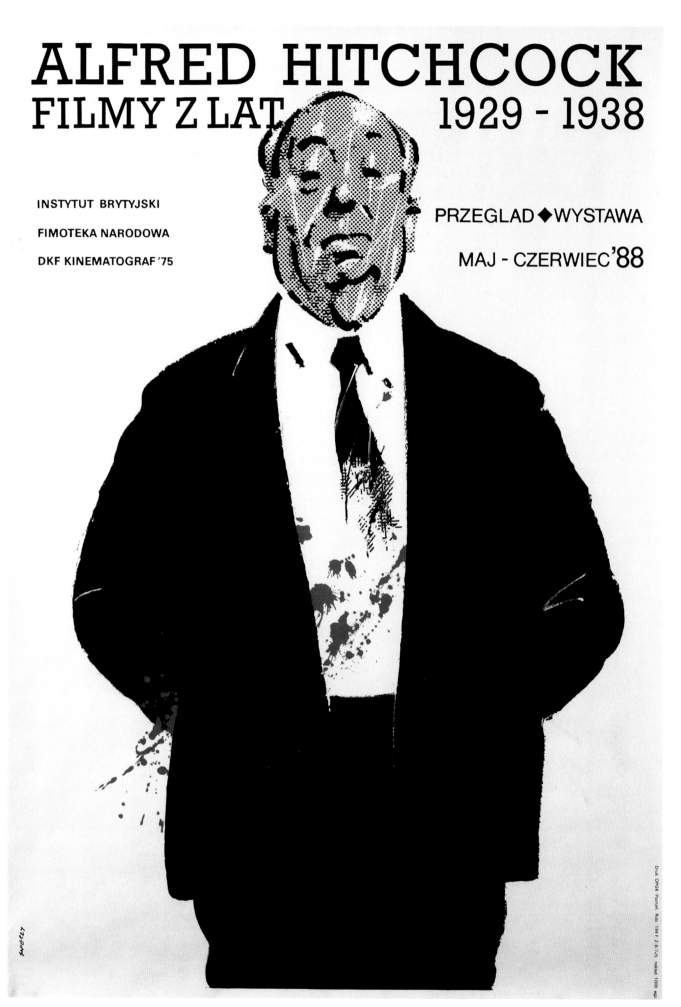

Hitchcock Film Festival (1929-1938) (1988)
Polish 38 x 26 in. (97 x 66 cm)
Art by Waldemar Swierzy

INDEX

ALSO AVAILABLE

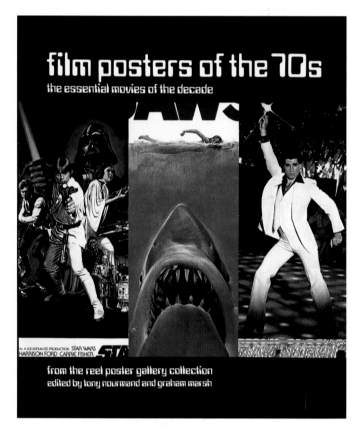

Film Posters of the 60s evokes the era when James Bond flicks were envelope-pushing fantasies for the bachelor-pad set.

NEWSWEEK

Here is a book which, for once, delivers just what you would expect from the title … For poster collectors – and everyone else – this is a crisp and stylish picture book.

DAILY MAIL

No commentary needed for this high-quality catalogue of the most evocative poster art of the decade taste forgot.

SIGHT AND SOUND

Film books naturally lend themselves to images and a really well-designed book of film poster art can prove contagiously entertaining and informative if only to discover how differently movies are marketed in other countries. **Film Posters of the 70s** does just what it says on the cover.

LONDON EVENING STANDARD